PEGASUS CHILDREN'S ENCYCLOPEDIA

FLOWERS

CONTENTS

What is a flower? 3

History 4

Parts of a flower 5

Types of flowers 9

Life cycle of flowers 12

Fertilization 13

Shapes of flowers 15

Colours of flowers 18

The symbolic meaning of flowers 19

Uses of flowers 20

Some well-known flowers 21

Test Your Memory 31

Index 32

What is a flower?

All plants produce flowers for the same reason— to make seeds so that another plant can grow.

Flowers are the reproductive structures produced by plants which belong to the group known as Angiosperms, or 'Flowering Plants'. This group includes an enormous variety of different plants ranging from buttercups and orchids to oak trees and grasses. There are about 250,000 known species.

Flowers are part of nearly every culture on Earth. There are thousands and thousands of flower species and people grow different types of flowers in gardens all over the world. Some types of flowers reproduce from bulbs, some from cuttings and some from seeds. Some types of flowers are perennials, meaning they do not have to be replanted every year, while some types are annuals. There are even types of flowers that are edible!

Tulips have a short lifespan of only three to seven days.

FLOWERS

History

Evidence of flowers dating back to the prehistoric period have been discovered through flower fossils. There are traces of association of flowers with humans during the Palaeolithic age.

People have used flowers to express their feelings, enhance their surroundings, and to celebrate important rituals and observances. All forms of art depict the use of flowers— music, books, paintings, sculpture, ceramics, tapestries, etc. Some of the most magnificent examples are the flower pictures produced by artists during the 17th, 18th and 19th centuries, which so accurately depict flowers and their incredible beauty.

Fossils of woody magnolia-like plants dating back 93 million years are the first evidence of plant life. More recently, tiny herb-like flower fossils dating back 120 million years have been uncovered by **Paleobotanists**.

Flowering plants, called angiosperms, were believed to be already diverse and found in most locations by the middle of the Cretaceous Period, 146 million years ago. A myriad of images of preserved flowers and flower parts have been found in fossils from Sweden, Portugal, England, and the United States.

Flower fossil

Astonishing fact

There are over 15,000 species of roses cultivated across the world!

Parts of a flower

Flower parts are usually arrayed in whorls (or cycles). There are commonly four distinct whorls of flower parts:

An outer **calyx** consisting of **sepals**; within it lies the **corolla**, consisting of **petals**; the **androecium**, or group of **stamens**; and in the centre is the **gynoecium**, consisting of the **pistils**.

Calyx

The calyx forms the outermost ring of a flower. Its component parts are the sepals. The sepals are generally green in colour.

Sepals give protection to the inner parts of the flower when the flower is in the bud condition.

Sepals form a sort of ring and enclose a developing flower bud. The calyx is made up of all the sepals together. Sometimes, sepal colours can be other than green and match the colour of the flower's petals or even be clear. But they are usually green.

calyx

Astonishing fact

Ancient civilizations believed that the smell of burning Aster leaves provided protection and drove away harmful serpents.

Corolla

The next ring on the receptacle (flower case) is called the **corolla**. It is composed of a few or many petals. The petals are typically showy and brightly coloured. They serve to attract pollinators for many species. Sometimes they are extremely fragrant. They may also exude nectar to reward the pollinator. Colour patterns might include nectar guides to point the way to the reward, or a 'bulls eye' target among the petals might get the flying pollinator to notice the flower.

The calyx and corolla are collectively called the **perianth**. A flower whose perianth is missing or either of these two whorls is called incomplete. A flower with both calyx and corolla has a complete perianth.

Within the corolla are one or more **stamens** containing pollen, which are the male reproductive structures. At the very centre of the flower are the female reproductive organs.

Astonishing fact

During the 1600s, Tulips were so valuable that their bulbs were worth more than gold!

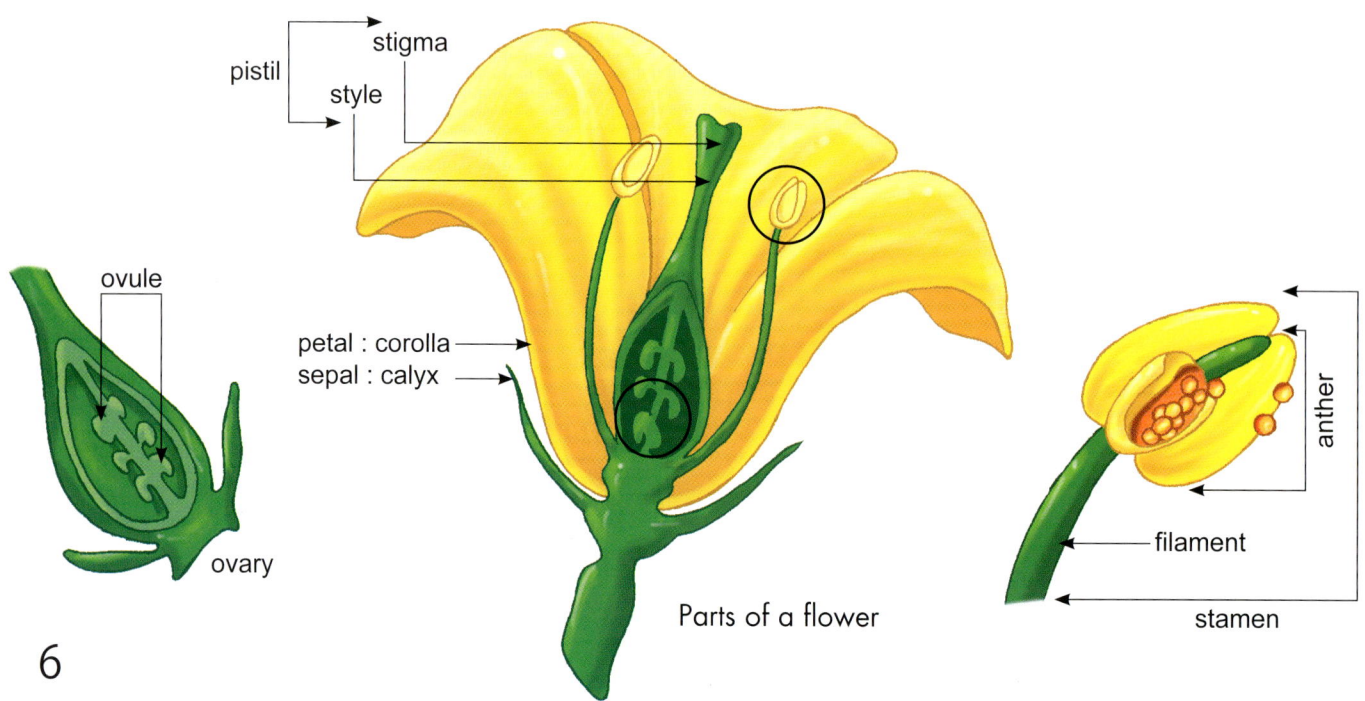

Parts of a flower

Parts of a flower

Androecium

The next whorl (ring) on the receptacle is called the **androecium**. It is the male reproductive part of the flower. It is composed of a few or many stamens. The stamens are specialized leaves with two distinct sections— the filament (a long stalk) and the anther (usually four sacs containing pollen grains). The function of the filament is to lift the anther to a position to effectively release pollen grains into/onto the pollinator. The filament also serves to provide the anther with xylem and phloem connections to the rest of the plant. The anther serves to produce pollen grains. The pollen grains ultimately make sperm cells, thus the idea of stamens as a male unit has come into being.

Astonishing fact

Tulip bulbs can be used in place of onions for cooking!

Gynoecium

The last whorl is the **gynoecium**, which is the female part of the plant. It is formed of a carpel, alternatively termed a pistil or carpels. The carpel consists of the style (with the stigma at its tip to receive pollen), the ovary and ovules, which have to be pollinated to produce seeds.

A flower may have one to many carpels, either fused or free. Each carpel is made up of the basal ovary, middle style and the upper stigma. The ovary is the chamber where there are many ovules that are attached to an axis. Each ovule consists of a haploid egg and other associated cells. The stigma is a sticky structure that receives the pollen grains. The style is hollow and provides a passage for the male gametes to reach the female gametes, the eggs.

Roses were considered the most sacred flowers in ancient Egypt and were used as offerings for the Goddess Isis. Roses have also been found in Egyptian tombs, where they were formed into funeral wreaths.

Types of flowers

There are different numerous parameters used in the classification of flowers. The anatomical arrangement of flower is known as the **morphology** of flower. Flowers are classified based on their morphology.

Classification on the basis of morphology

- **Sympetalous**: The petals of these flowers are joined, either partially or fully

- **Polypetalous**: The petals of these flowers are not joined

- **Actinomorphic**: Most flowers are actinomorphic, meaning they can be divided into 3 or more identical sectors which are related to each other by rotation about the centre of the flower. Typically, each sector would contain one petal, one sepal and so on. Actinomorphic flowers are also called radially symmetrical or regular flowers. Other examples of actinomorphic flowers are the lily and the buttercup.

- **Zygomorphic**: Zygomorphic flowers can be divided by only a single plane into two mirror-image halves, much like a person's face. Examples are orchids and the flowers of most members of the Lamiales. Zygomorphic flowers generally have petals of two more different shapes, sizes and colours.

Astonishing fact

Lilies are believed to have been under cultivation longer than any other flower, having existed in gardens 3,000 years ago.

FLOWERS

Classification on the basis of flower branches, clusters and inflorescences

- **Single flower**: Single flowers are present at the tip of peduncle, an elongated stalk or branch of the main axis of the plant. Tulip and Magnolia grandiflora are such examples.

- **Cluster**: Under this category, three or more flowers are found gathered in close formation, in simple or branched manner. Ligustrum japonicum, firethorn and Sweet William are examples of flowers under this category.

- **Inflorescence**: The arrangement of flowers or groups of flowers is termed as **inflorescence**. Different flowers are grouped differently, but some characteristics are same for certain flower types, which help in identifying their species. These are further classified into two categories— racemose type and cymose type.

In racemose inflorescences, the axis grows continuously and the oldest flower is borne at the base, while the newest one is seen near the growing tip. In cymose inflorescences, the upward growth of the floral axis stops with the development of terminal flower, the oldest flower is borne at the tip, while the younger one appears lower down on the axis.

> The Netherlands is the world's leading exporter of Roses.

Classification on the basis of position

- **Terminal**: Flowers under this category can be seen either as singles or in groups on the ends of the axis or branches. Examples are Magnolia grandiflora and Nerium oleander.
- **Axillary**: Here, flowers and clusters of flowers can be found at the junction of the stem or axis and the leaf. Examples are periwinkle, beautyberry and hibiscus.

Classification on the basis of blossom

- **Annual flowers**: Plants that flower or ripen their seeds or fruits in the same season in which they are sown are called annuals. They are further classified into hardy and half-hardy or tender kinds.
- **Biennial flowers**: These are plants that do not flower during the first growing season and die after the second season; that is, they are in perfection in only one season.
- **Perennials**: These plants continue to produce brilliant flowers for several years in succession. The most common of them is the rose that is grown in thorny bushes.

> Japan has a national chrysanthemum festival every year on September 9. This flower is also portrayed on their imperial flags and weapons.

Life cycle of flowers

Pollination

In angiosperms, pollination is the transfer of pollen from an anther to a stigma. Pollen grains land on the sticky stigma, where they begin to germinate or grow. A pollen tube then forms down the style, sperm is delivered to the ovules and fertilization takes place.

Pollination by wind

Many angiosperms are pollinated by wind. Wind-pollinated flowers, such as those of corn and all grasses, tend to have a simple structure lacking petals. The anthers dangle on long filaments, allowing the light pollen grains to be easily caught by the wind. The stigma is freely exposed to catch the airborne pollen.

Pollination by animals

In general, pollination by insects and other animals is more efficient than pollination by wind. The flowers of many species of plants are marked with special pigments that absorb ultraviolet light (light whose wavelengths are shorter than visible light). These pigments are invisible to humans and most animals. But the eyes of bees are sensitive enough to detect the patterns created by the pigments and so the bees are drawn to them.

Having been attracted to a flower, an insect or other small animal probe inside for its reward. In doing so, it brushes against the anthers and picks up dust pollen on its body. When the animal moves on to the next flower, it brushes past the stigma depositing the pollen.

Chrysanthemum blooms can be as small as 1 cm or as large as 25 cm.

Fertilization

Once, a pollen grain reaches the stigma of another flower of the same species, it will produce a pollen tube. This grows down through the style until it reaches an ovule. Fertilization then takes place resulting in a seed.

When pollen from one flower fertilizes the ovule of another flower, it is called **cross pollination**. If an ovule is fertilized by pollen from the same flower, it is called self fertilization. In evolutionary terms, this is generally not particularly favourable, as it leads to inbreeding. Most species therefore tend to be cross pollinated. In this case, they need something to transfer the pollen from one flower to another. This might be insects, birds, wind or water. This need to use an outside agent to transfer the pollen has led to the extraordinary variety of shapes, colours, scents and arrangements of flowers seen today.

The seed

A flower's fertilized eggs become seeds, while its ovary wall becomes the fruit that contains them. Rose hips are one example. Each seed is surrounded by a tough, protective coating containing food for the growing plant. A layer called the endosperm stores short-term nutrients, while the long-term supply is stored in two cotyledons that may resemble lima beans in shape.

Seeds

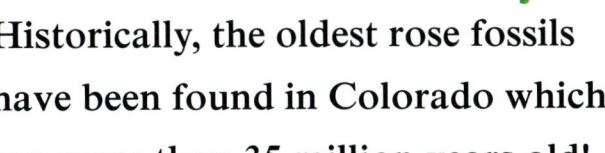

Astonishing fact

Historically, the oldest rose fossils have been found in Colorado which are more than 35 million years old!

Seed dispersal

Seed dispersal serves several important functions. It limits overcrowding, helps seeds spread out into new areas and eases competition between the seeds and parent plant. Animals help with dispersal when they eat flowers or fruit and later excrete the seeds in their waste. Wind and water can also carry seeds away. Some plants 'self-disperse,' for instance, bursting in the hot sun to shoot the seeds in all directions.

Growth

Once a seed finds favourable conditions it begins to germinate or grow. The future root extends downward into the soil while the future shoot reaches upward for sunlight. Leaves form and begin to carry out photosynthesis while roots absorb necessary water and minerals.

Photosynthesis allows a plant to make its own food in the form of sugar. All that is required for this process is light, carbon dioxide, water and sunlight. Veins in the leaves help transport water and nutrients throughout the plant as needed.

Finally, buds form to protect the developing flowers. Mature flowers unravel, complete with petals and the male and female reproductive organs. Pollen is produced, and the life cycle begins again.

Astonishing fact
There are more than 25,000 varieties of daffodils!

Shapes of flowers

Bell-shaped

Bell-shaped flowers are properly known as campanulate blooms. The common characteristics include wide tubes fringed by flared petal tips. Campanulate enthusiasts often fill their gardens with flowers like bleeding hearts, Carolina silver bells, southern catalpa and English bluebells.

Bleeding hearts

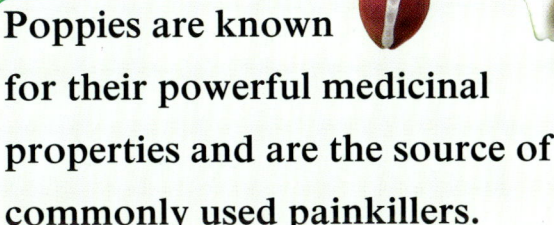

Poppies are known for their powerful medicinal properties and are the source of commonly used painkillers.

English bluebells

Trumpet

Trumpet-shaped flowers begin with a narrow, tubular base and gradually flare into a widened mouth. Petals at the end of trumpet flowers often fold back onto themselves. Trumpet vines are a popular variety of this particular flower shape, as is the petunia. Other examples include Incarvillea grandiflora and Brugmansia.

Incarvillea grandiflora

FLOWERS

Funnel-shaped

Funnel-shaped flowers have a narrow base and gradually widen in a flared or open shape. Examples of funnel-shaped flowers are morning glory, Peruvian lily, primrose, forget-me-nots, freesia, gardenia, hibiscus, hollyhock and mallow.

Morning glory

Star-shaped

The petals of a star-shaped flower each protrude separately from a central point on the blossom. Petals of star-shaped flowers typically range in number from five to nine. Common star flower varieties include the Star of Bethlehem, Tabaco cimarron and water jasmine.

Star-shaped flower

Freesia

Cross-shaped

When a flower has four petals that are arranged to form the shape of an 'X' or cross, it is known as a **cruciform flower**. One of the most common examples of this shape would be the dogwood tree's blooms. However, this is not the only place where cruciform flowers can be found. Flowering plants within the family Brassicaceae (radish, cauliflower, mustard, etc.) are commonly referred to as crucifers due to the prevalence of cross-shaped blooms.

Cross-shaped flower

Astonishing fact

The starfish flower has the appearance and odour of a piece of rotting flesh in the shape of a starfish.

Shapes of flowers

Anemone flowers

Saucer-shaped

Flowers with a saucer shape typically feature petals that extend almost straight outward, sometimes curling up slightly at the tips. Plants that feature saucer-shaped blooms include sunflowers, saucer magnolia, anemone flowers and asters.

Saucer magnolia

Asters

Tubular-shaped

The defining characteristic of tubular flowers is a series of united petals which form a long, narrow tube. Often, though not always, the united petals will separate at the end of the bloom, providing a small flare. These unique-shaped blossoms are frequently seen among flowering shrubs in the desert areas.

Tubular flowers

Astonishing fact

The Iris flower is name after Iris, the Goddess of the Rainbow. The Iris flower occur in shades of blue, purple, white, yellow, pink, orange, brown, red and black.

Colours of flowers

Flowers come in many different colours. The colour of a flower often influences the type of pollinator that visits it. Bees are able to see ultraviolet light, a 'colour' that humans can't see. Many flowers reflect ultraviolet light. Some flowers have ultraviolet nectar guides. They 'glow' like neon signs in a field!

Red and orange flowers attract hummingbirds. Bees can't see red or orange.

Blue, yellow and white flowers attract bees and butterflies. Maroon flowers attract flies and some beetles. Green flowers are usually, but not always, wind pollinated.

Astonishing fact

The Underground Orchid lives entirely underground! Unlike other plants, this unique orchid cannot use sunlight to obtain its energy and instead gets its food from the decaying stumps of another plant, the broom honey myrtle.

The symbolic meaning of flowers

People throughout various cultures and lands have been drawn to the beauty and fragrance of flowers. From ancient times until today, flowers have been used for adornment and to express intimate feelings.

Flowers are often associated with spring and rebirth. They represent renewal, youth and beauty. Flowers are also symbolic of the eternal cycle of life and death. Flowers are associated with numerous occasions and events. They are presented on birthdays, anniversaries and holidays. They are used to celebrate joyous occasions such as weddings and also to express sympathy during sad events such as funerals. The use of flowers in events such as these signifies the symbolism of flowers in the cycle of life and death.

The symbolism of flowers is often determined both by colour and type. Generally, white is symbolic of purity and innocence. Red represents passion and love. Pink also symbolizes love as well as happiness, beauty and friendship. Yellow is associated with purity, truth and intellect whereas orange is symbolic of warmth, creativity and growth. Green also represents growth as well as hope, renewal and fertility. Blue is a symbol of peace, tranquillity and healing while purple represents devotion, faith, nobility and spirituality.

Uses of flowers

Flowers are not just beautiful to look at, but they also serve a vital role in our ecosystem. Flowers attract insects and birds, which serve as pollinators for the plant itself. Insects and birds also help keep the surrounding ecosystem of flowers well maintained and healthy by keeping away predators, and utilizing the plants or flowers for their own growth. Flowers help keep the ecosystem growing and provide new plant life, as well as help sustain local insects and birds.

In addition to the benefits flowers provide to the local ecosystem, they also greatly benefit humans. The bugs and birds that the flowers attract help in keeping our environment healthy. The seeds that flowers drop and pollinate locally producing more plants, more fruits and vegetables for us to eat. In addition, certain bugs such as bees, produce honey from the nectar of the flowers, but also pollinate the flowers as they do so, allowing them to produce seeds.

Without insects or birds, there would have no way of reproducing to create new flowers or growth. Flowers help our ecosystem flourish and attract a plethora of life to the area and facilitate the expansion of our environment. If flowers are cut down or destroyed before pollination can occur, that particular species has a high chance of dying off in that area. In addition, local wildlife will also vanish in that area since they would have no food.

Some well-known flowers

Parrot Flower

The parrot flower is a very rare species discovered in the Shan States of Upper Burma by A.H. Hildebrand, a British official. It is one of nature's most beautiful creations. A rare plant and a protected species, Thai government has banned export of its seeds or plants.

A marvellous creation of divine, it has combined the parrot and the flower. The flower in the shape of a parrot in flight grows approx six feet in height. It blossoms in October and November and grows in tropical, humid and moist conditions.

These plants are rare members the of impatiens psittacina –the botanical name of the plants. The word psittacina when translated means 'parrot like'. It is difficult to cultivate for it needs a local natural pollinator to produce seeds.

The species grows in the wild in a small region of north Thailand (near Chiang Mai), Burma, and in the north-east Indian state of Manipur. It is called the parrot flower because its flower bears a resemblance to a parrot in flight when viewed from the side.

FLOWERS

Kadupul Flower

The legendary flower, named Kadupul is native to Sri Lanka. The Kadupul flower blooms rarely and only at night – mysteriously; the flower withers before dawn.

Seeing Kadupul flower bloom is a very rare experience among those that grow the flower. Kadupul flower is native to Sri Lankan lands but still, the blooming of the flowers has rarely been spotted even by the locals.

This epiphytic plant grows in the branches of large trees, where the decayed particles of bark and moisture collect to give it a rich protective foothold. The plant has leathery leaves and the leaves are long with scalloped (designed) edges. The scallops point downwards. During November to March, a little shoot appears at the point where two scallops meet; the shoot grows to a length of about five inches before it bears a bud, which hangs down on its slender stem.

Some well-known flowers

Wolffia

It not only holds the record of the world's smallest flower, but also world smallest fruit. Wolffia arrhiza produces the world's smallest flower. It also produces the smallest fruit called utricle. These plants grow floating in still or slow moving water. They are commonly referred as duckweed or Water-meal.

Each plant is shaped like a microscope football with a flat or rounded top depending upon the species. These plants have a freely floating body with no stem or leaf, and are green to yellow in colour. An average individual plant is 0.6 mm long, 0.3 mm wide.

Each plant produces a minute flower in the cavity present in the upper part of the plant body. A flower of this plant has only one single pistil and stamen. A bouquet of a dozen such plants in full bloom will occupy no more space then a pinhead.

FLOWERS

Rafflesia Arnoldii

Rafflesia, a native of rainforests of Sumatra and Borneo in the Indonesian Archipelago, is the largest flower in the world. The flower has a diameter of around one metre and can weigh up to 11 kg.

It produces no leaves, stems or roots but lives as a parasite on the **Tetrastigma** vine, which grows only in primary (undisturbed) rainforest. Only the flower or bud can be seen; the rest of the plant exists only as filaments within its host. The blossom is pollinated by flies attracted by its scent, which resembles that of decaying flesh.

The Rafflesia is rare and fairly hard to locate. It is especially difficult to see in bloom. The buds take many months to develop and the blossom lasts for just a few days. How many of these strange plants still survive is unknown.

Some well-known flowers

Titan Arum

The Titan arum is a species of plant known by the scientific name Amorphophallus titanum. It is also known by the common name 'bunga bangkai' in Sumatra, which is translated as 'corpse flower' because of its smell of rotten egg and fish. It was first discovered by an Italian botanist named Odoardo Beccari.

The Titan arum has the largest inflorescence (groups of leaves; compound flower) in the world. The inflorescence reaches 2 m tall; taller than a man. The native habitat of this species is only Sumatra, Indonesia. This wonderful creature is an autotroph— a plant that performs photosynthesis process to obtain its own food for survival.

The corpse flower is also believed to be one of the stinkiest flowers in the world, having the strongest odour the first night or first two evenings after blooming. According to some observers, the scent seems to hold resemblance to rotten fish, which is caused by sulfur compounds, also contained in rotten eggs, providing the flower its smell.

Lily of the Valley

The Lily of the Valley has originated in Europe. Today it is distributed widely throughout North America and North Asia, but in England it is still found as commonly as wild flowers. It is a small, bell-shaped flower that gives off a large scent that attracts not only people, but bees who like to collect the pollen that the flower produces.

The flowers are normally white, although occasionally you can find some with a pink hue to them. The flower first grows in the spring and creates six little stamens. By September, the flower produces sweet berries in place of the petals that are about 5-7mm in diameter.

The Lily of the Valley has some medicinal qualities to it. For many years the leaves and petals have been used in medicine because they contain cardiac glycosides.

The Lily of the Valley is also known as **Our Lady's Tears** because according to the legend the tears that that Mary shed at the cross turned into Lily of the Valley flowers.

Astonishing fact

Lilies produce large quantities of pollen. To remove pollen from clothes lightly brush off the pollen with a toothbrush; this will prevent staining.

Some well-known flowers

Roses

Roses, popularly known as the queen of flowers look beautiful and spread fragrance in any garden. This regal flowering shrub valued mainly for the colour and fragrance of their flowers, has about 150 species. Many thousands of roses have been developed through cross breeding, selection and hybridization. Rose plants range in size from compact, miniature roses, to climbers that can reach 7 m in height.

The rose has been a symbol of love, beauty, even war and politics from way back in time. The variety, colour and even number of roses carry symbolic meanings. The rose is most popularly known as the flower of love.

Rose flowers are a perennial species, which implies they come back annually. They are often discovered on shrubs or vines and are typically very fragrant. They are finicky growers and do not like standing water. Rose flowers grow finest in full sunlight. They require to be fed through fertilization at least once in a season and thrive beneath fixed pruning and care. Most are native to Asia, with smaller numbers of species native to Europe, North America, and northwest Africa.

27

Ixora flowers

The Ixora is a common ornamental flower throughout tropical areas and comes in a variety of colours and species. Commonly known as **West Indian Jasmine**, the Ixora is a genus of 529 species in the Rubiaceae family, which consists of tropical evergreen trees and shrubs. Though native to the tropics and subtropics, its centre of diversity is in tropical areas in Asia, especially India.

Plants are of two types— large with the height around 1 m, and dwarf or miniature plants. Miniature ones have small leaves and are bushy. The Ixora produces flowers, even when only a few inches high and is commonly used as a small garden plant. Plants possess leathery leaves, ranging from 3 to 6 inches in length and produce large clusters of tiny flowers. Red Ixora flowers are commonly used in Hindu worship, as well as in Indian folk medicine.

Some well-known flowers

Orchids

The orchid family, Orchidaceae, is the most numerous in the plant kingdom. There are about 25,000 to 30,000 known species of orchids around the world. Orchids are found in all continents except Antarctica, from hot tropical jungles to the cold climate in North America. However, some orchids are found only in certain region of the world and nowhere else, for example, the Vanda genus colonizes only South East Asia.

Orchid flowers have an array of varying colours, fragrances and habitats. The fragrance of an orchid can be sweet or foul. Orchid flowers are shaped differently too; there are orchid slippers, orchid buckets and orchid helmets.

Orchid flowers differ from the majority of flower species in both their pollination systems and structural make-up. The male and female parts of the orchid are actually fused together and located to one side of the flower. Orchids have long periods of pollination as the chance of an orchid being pollinated is minimal. Orchids rely on insects for pollination, although some species of orchids are capable of self-pollination.

As forest dwelling plants, many orchids grow as 'epiphytes', which means that they grow on the trees, clinging on with thick aerial roots and storing water in either fleshy leaves or thickened stems called **pseudobulbs**. There are also many orchids that grow in the ground. These are known as **terrestrials**.

FLOWERS

Cherry Blossom

The cherry blossom (Sakura) is Japan's unofficial national flower. It has been celebrated for many centuries and holds a very prominent position in Japanese culture.

There are many dozens of different cherry tree varieties in Japan, most of which bloom for just a couple of days in spring. The Japanese celebrate that time of the year with hanami (cherry blossom viewing) parties under the blooming trees.

Cherry Blossom is native to the Himalayas and is found in East Asia such as China, Korea and Japan. It is an ornamental tree and includes Prunus serrulata, and their blossoms.

Japan's most beloved variety of cherry blossom is the Somei Yoshino. Its flowers are nearly pure white, tinged with the palest pink, especially near the stem. The flowers bloom, and usually fall within a week, before the leaves come out. Therefore, the trees look nearly white from top to bottom. This variety of cherry blossom takes its name from the village of Somei.

Test Your MEMORY

1. Define flowers.

2. Write briefly about the history of flowers.

3. Name the parts of a flower.

4. Name the types of flowers.

5. Describe the lifecycle of a flower.

6. What is pollination?

7. Describe the different shapes of flowers.

8. Write two lines about the colour of flowers.

9. Write about the uses of flowers.

10. Write briefly about the Parrot flower.

11. Which flower is the symbol of love?

12. Which family of flowers is the most numerous in the plant kingdom?

Index

A

actinomorphic 9
androecium 5, 7
angiosperms 3, 4, 12
annual flowers 11
anther 7, 12
autotroph 25

B

biennial flowers 11

C

calyx 5, 6
campanulate blooms 15
carpel 8
cluster 10
corolla 5, 6
cross pollination 13
cruciform flower 16

E

edible 3

F

filaments 12, 24
flower fossils 4

G

germinate 12, 14
gynoecium 5, 8

I

inflorescence 10, 25

M

morphology 9

O

ovary 8, 13
ovules 8, 12

P

Paleobotanists 4
perennials 3, 11
perianth 6
petals 5, 6, 9, 12, 14, 15, 16, 17, 26
phloem 7
photosynthesis 14, 25
pistils 5
pollen grains 7, 8, 12, 13
pollen tube 12, 13
pollination 12, 13, 20, 29
pollinators 6, 20
polypetalous 9
pseudobulbs 29

S

seeds 3, 8, 11, 13, 14, 20, 21
sepals 5
single flower 10
species 3, 4, 6, 10, 12, 13, 20, 21, 23, 25, 27, 28, 29
sperm 7, 12
stamens 5, 6, 7, 26
stigma 6, 8, 12, 13
style 6, 8, 12, 13
sympetalous 9

T

terrestrials 29

X

xylem 7

Z

zygomorphic 9